ב"ה

RAV DOVBER PINSON

THE FOUR SPECIES

*The Symbolism of the Lulav & Esrog
and Intentions for the Lulav Movements*

IYYUN PUBLISHING

THE FOUR SPECIES © 2012 Dovber Pinson.
All rights reserved. No part of this book may be used or reproduced in any manner whatsoever without written permission except in the case of brief quotations embedded in critical articles and reviews.

Published by IYYUN Publishing
232 Bergen Street
Brooklyn, NY 11217

www.IYYUN.com

Iyyun Publishing books may be purchased for educational, business or sales promotional use. For information please contact: contact@IYYUN.com

cover image: courtesy of Hidur Gallery, Israel www.Hidur.com
cover and book design: Rochie Pinson
illustrations for lulav movements: Elke Sudin

pb ISBN 978-0-9852011-4-2
Pinson, DovBer 1971-
The Four Species: The symbolism of the Lulav and Esrog and Intentions for the Lulav Movements/ DovBer Pinson

1. Judaism 2. Spirituality 3. Holidays

RAV DOVBER PINSON

THE FOUR SPECIES

*The Symbolism of the Lulav & Esrog
and Intentions for the Lulav Movements*

IYYUN PUBLISHING

contents

INTRODUCTION *2*

CHAPTER 1

BEAUTIFUL FRUIT OF THE TREE:
THE DEEPER SYMBOLISM OF THE FOUR SPECIES *10*

CHAPTER 2

UNITY IN MOTION:
INTENTION IN WAVING THE FOUR SPECIES *32*

CHAPTER 3

HOW TO PERFORM THE NA'ANUIM *49*

CHAPTER 4

THE ILLUSTRATED GUIDE TO WAVING THE LULAV *52*

CHAPTER 5

KAVANOS, INTENTIONS 1 & 2 *56*

{ SPECIAL THANKS TO: }

MR. YECHIEL (ILYA) GOLD שיחי'

MR. YAAKOV ELKAN שיחי'

MR. ZEV DRIZIN שיחי'

For their continued support and the sponsorship of this book

Shefa Berachos Gashmi V'Ruchni
An abundance of physical and spiritual blessings

Introduction

the cycle of the calendar is a curriculum of sorts — a spiritual curriculum designed to lead us through the alternating ascents and descents of the human soul as it winds its way back to Oneness.

Along this journey through time, one encounters all relevant stages along the path of individuation, disintegration, and integration: exile, wandering, homecoming, harvest, destruction and rededication, liberation, revelation, reflection, and ultimately rebirth.

The calendar is both a path to be traveled, as well as the carriage that carries us along the course of this journey. By consciously engaging the calendar we can jump into the flow of time and transformation as it dips and rises through the year, navigating the unpredictable currents of consciousness all the way back to the Source of the river.

It is not within the scope of this book to outline in detail the full trajectory of the human soul as it is represented in the narrative of the calendar, but suffice it to say for our purposes that the end of one year (Elul), and the beginning of the next year (Tishrei), is a major crux of the process.

Elul begins the time when we are approaching the next big phase of our journey and so, just like the ancient Israelites on the banks of the Jordan recalled with Moshe the high and low points of their journey in the book of *Devarim*, or Deuteronomy, we too reflect, refine, and take stock of our past experiences. This is the time to 'pay any outstanding bills' or 'repair any damaged goods' due to the wear and tear of our soul's journey through the last year.

This is the process known as *Cheshbon HaNefesh*, an accounting of the soul.

Tishrei then signals the initiation of the next cycle.

This is where we recalibrate our internal compass and take the first tentative steps out of the womb of reflection and into the big, wide world with a clean slate. Where we hear, as if for the first time, the startled cry of a newborn in the sound of the Shofar, where we are held and learn to trust the wings of the Shechinah in the temporary structure of the Sukkah, and where we lift up, dance with, and kiss the Torah in the joy of renewal that we experience on Simchas Torah.

There are many metaphors to characterize this crucial turning point along the course of the calendar. One potent analogy is that of a cosmic or spiritual wedding in which our soul is (re)-united with the Most High. Seen in this light, the process begun in Elul, and climaxing in Tishrei, comes to life in a vivid and visceral way.

Let's explore this metaphor a little deeper.

The culmination of the month of Tishrei is an experience of spiritual intimacy, and closeness with our Creator. In preparation for this awesome encounter, first we must traverse the month of Elul, in which we cultivate a state of *Besulah*, or youthful innocence. Rosh Hashanah is like a *Tenayim*, or engagement ceremony, in which we make a formal commitment to our Divine 'Fiancé'. On Yom Kippur we call out with abandon, 'I love You, I want to be with You, I want to feel Your presence at every moment!'

Finally, we reach Sukkos and enter under the chupah, where we 'marry' Hashem.

INTRODUCTION

We celebrate our union in the *Sukkah* for seven days, like the *Sheva B'rachos*, the seven days of blessing and rejoicing with a groom and bride. The sukkah is also like Hashem's embrace—the halachic minimum for a kosher sukkah is three walls (two whole walls and a portion of a third), and these form a chest, an upper arm and forearm, which hold us intimately. We are one in this embrace.

In this state of spiritual intimacy, we affectionately remember Rosh Hashanah and Yom Kippur, and we desire to internalize these experiences in a way that can make them eternal. By going out into the sukkah, we declare to our Beloved, 'I am ready to go wherever You want me to go—even to a tent, out in the cold—so long as I will be one with You forever.'

This is one clear meditative intention behind sitting in a sukkah for seven days. The most basic *kavanah* is actually explicit in the Torah: "…In order that your generations will know that I caused the Children of Israel to dwell in sukkos when I brought them forth from the land of Egypt" *[Vayikra, 23:43]*.

Throughout this festival we follow another Divine request as well: "You shall take...the beautiful fruit of the tree, a palm branch, myrtle branches, and willow branches from the stream, and rejoice before Hashem your G-d for seven days" *[Vayikra, 23:40]*. What is the purpose and intention behind gathering these plants, and how does this motivate us to "rejoice before Hashem"?

Torah wisdom is concerned with a deep wound we all carry. Despite the fact that *ein od mil'vado*—there is nothing but Hashem, and Divine Oneness pervades all directions and dimensions—we feel ourselves thrust into a fractured world, where there is a conflict between reality as it is perceived, and reality as it is. However, something inside us always remembers Oneness. This subtle recognition draws us toward piercing the veils and seeing beyond the appearance of separation. Our deepest desire is spiritual intimacy with our Source, in every act and detail of our lives.

For seven days a year, we are given a tremendous gift. The Torah gives us the *arba minim*, the 'Four Species', as spiritual tools that can empower us to fully pierce the veils in our lives—to remove all separation, negativity and obstacles to the perception of Divine Unity. With these tools, we can channel the experience of Oneness into our mundane lives. We can make the intimacy eternal.

However, before we can summon this full transformational power, we must prepare our meditative intentionality, our kavannah. We must understand the multiple layers of symbolism in the arba minim, and the *naanuim,* the waving ritual.

The first section of this book, entitled **Beautiful Fruit of the Tree: The Deeper Symbolism of the Four Species** is a wide survey of the meanings and context of the arba minim. The second section, entitled **Unity in Motion: Intention in Waving the Four Species,** is a guide to transformative kavannah.

In these chapters, you will learn to take the power of the Four Species into your hands, and use them for personal development and deeper spiritual awareness. You can gain the ability to make Divine Unity an intimate, real, and lasting experience in your life. This, indeed, will be reason to "rejoice before Hashem."

Beautiful Fruit of the Tree:
The Deeper Symbolism of the Four Species

ARBA MINIM, THE FOUR SPECIES

Regarding Sukkos, the Torah tells us, "You shall take...the beautiful fruit of the tree (the esrog or 'citron'), a palm branch (lulav), myrtle branches (hadasim) and willow branches (aravos) from the stream, and rejoice before Hashem your G-d for seven days" *[Vayikra, 23:40].*

Collectively, the *esrog, lulav, hadasim* and *aravos* are called the *arba minim,* the 'Four Kinds' or Four Species. The latter three plants are neatly bundled together, and on each day of Sukkos (except Shabbos) we take them in our hands, make a blessing over them, and then, along with the esrog, we wave or move them in a series of spatial directions.

Before we can properly explore the purpose and intention of waving the arba minim, we need to understand why we select these four species in particular, and what each one symbolizes.

The Torah itself only tells us to 'take' these four species and rejoice—it offers no explicit reason for doing this. The truth is, we do not need graspable reasons for the mitzvos, for they are rooted in the absolute simplicity of Hashem's Unity, and reasons suggest something extraneous to this simple Unity. On the other hand, we are fashioned by our Creator to seek meaning and also to think and function in a binary mode, making sense through reason and intuition, contrast and correspondence, physical form and mystical symbol, and history and dream of the future. Therefore, while keeping Unity in mind, we also explore the ethical, philosophical and mystical reasons for the mitzvos, including the arba minim.

We can organize these reasons into four or five categories known by their acronym, **PaRDeS**:

1) *Peshat*, literal interpretation

2) *Remez*, allegorical interpretation

3) *Derush*, homiletic meaning

4) *Sod*, secret or Kabbalistic meaning

5) *Sod shebeSod*, secret within the secret.

Let us now discuss the **PaRDeS** of why we gather the Four Species.

PESHAT: LITERAL INTERPRETATION

The Rambam writes a *peshat*, or interpretation that Sukkos is a joyous Yom Tov because it is the time of gathering produce from the fields.*[Morah, 3: 43]* The Torah calls this festival *Chag ha-Asif*, the Festival of Gathering, or harvest festival, and explains, "After the gathering of your threshing floor and vat, you shall hold the Feast of Sukkos for seven days" *[Devarim, 16:13]*.

Another peshat is that we are commemorating the sukkos, or booths, that we sat in during our forty-year journey through the desert. The Torah says that we should sit in a sukkah "...in order that your generations may know that I caused the Children of Israel to dwell in booths when I brought them out of the land of Egypt" *[Vayikra, 23:43]*. According to a literal reading, we can say these sukkos were either literal booths, or they were representations of the Clouds of Glory that protected the Children of Israel on their journeys.

CONTEXT

While the primary peshat reason for the Yom Tov is the historical narrative (content) – recalling the sitting in the clouds of Glory or the tents as we left Egypt and journeyed in the desert – it can also be understood within a particular seasonal context. The seasonal context of Sukkos is a time of harvesting and gathering produce from the fields. The deeper understanding of this peshat is that on Sukkos we gather or assimilate into our lives all the inspiration that we experienced from Rosh Hashanah through Yom Kippur. Taking the enthusiasm of commitment we have experienced during Rosh Hashanah –Yom Kippur and now moving under the *Chupa*. First come the days of awe, where we turn to Hashem and say; I love you Hashem, I want to live differently, I am committed to You and to my spiritual development, and than comes Sukkos were we actually go under the Chupa with Hashem, as it were.

The Rambam says the Torah instructs us to gather these four types of vegetation in our hand because Sukkos is related to gathering vegetation from the fields, a harvest celebration. The reasons for these specific four plants are

- a) they are four species that are found throughout the Land of Israel
- b) they are aesthetically pleasant
- c) they do not wither quickly, so they are durable enough to remain intact for the duration of the seven day Yom Tov.

These four different species also originate from four basic natural environments in the Land of Israel, the desert, the coast, the mountains and the rivers. The lulav comes from the palm tree, which grows in the desert, and the esrog fruit grows in the coastal plains. Hadasim come from myrtle trees, which grow in the mountainous regions, and the aravos come from willow trees, which grow in riverbeds. Therefore, the context of the Four Species suggests that gathering them together symbolizes gathering and unifying all areas of the Holy Land.

CHAPTER ONE

THE SEASON OF JOY

"You shall take... the beautiful fruit of the tree, a palm branch, myrtle twigs and willow...and rejoice before Hashem your G-d for seven days"[Vayikra, 23:40].

The Four Species are literally connected with Rejoicing before Hashem.

When the harvest arrives, one reaps the benefits of his hard labor and receives the produce that will be used throughout the winter months. Therefore, it is a naturally joyous time. The *Chinuch* says that the Torah tells us to celebrate "before Hashem your G-d for seven days" *(Mitzvah 324)* because instead of rejoicing in our physical abundance alone, we are to take this time to thank and praise Hashem, the Source of life's blessings. When we direct our physical joy toward Hashem, we can transform it into spiritual joy. According to the Chinuch, this is the peshat of the reason that we take physical objects in our hands during our spiritual service.

Since the lulav, esrog, hadasim, and aravos, are objects of a mitzvah, they remind to us to be joyful and thankful before the Creator, Who gave us the mitzvah. Also, these objects bring joy in themselves, in the words of the *Chinuch*: "All four species gladden the hearts of those who see them." So beyond being prevalent throughout the land, durable, and aesthetically pleasant, they also inspire joy to those who behold them.

NATURE'S ARRAY

Expanding on the seasonal context of Sukkos, Rav Shimshon Raphael Hirsh writes that since this festival is a celebration of nature, we hold these four species, which together express a full array of the wonders of nature. This array is expressed through four different elemental categories: naturally occurring substances that

1) have both a beautiful aroma and a satisfying taste
2) have a pleasant taste, but no aroma
3) have a beautiful aroma but no taste
4) have neither an aroma nor taste.

CHAPTER ONE

THE ESROG:

The first category is represented by the esrog. There are some natural phenomena in our lives that do not require any human processing in order to extract their benefit. They come ready-made; we could call them transparent or perfect. 'Aromatic' alludes to anything that benefits life through spiritual beauty and abstract enjoyment, while 'tasty' alludes to anything that benefits us through more tangible forms of satisfaction or nourishment. The esrog thus symbolizes all the things that Hashem gives us that are effortlessly and perfectly transparent to the Divine satisfaction.

THE LULAV:

The second category is represented by the lulav, which contains a tasty or nourishing substance but has no striking aroma. There are many natural phenomena that give us satisfaction in life, but have no outstanding spiritual beauty. We usually have to process these phenomena to extract their benefit, as is frequently the case with plants that are used for food.

THE HADASIM:

The third category is represented by the hadasim, the

myrtle twigs, which have a fragrant aroma but are inedible. Similarly, many natural phenomena benefit us simply by means of their beautiful appearance or spiritual qualities, yet we would not take a bite out of them, as it were, nor would they satisfy our taste.

THE ARAVOS:

The fourth category is represented by the aravos or willow branches, which contain no aroma and are inedible. These represent natural substances that provide only the raw materials and basic requirements of life, such as a physical place to live and utilitarian articles of clothing.

By gathering together these four elements in the form of the arba minim, we show gratitude and praise to Hashem for all of nature's gifts.

SPECIES	FORM OF BENEFIT / INDUCEMENT TO PRAISE
ESROG	TRANSPARENCY
LULAV	SATISFACTION
HADASIM	BEAUTY
ARAVOS	UTILITY

CHAPTER ONE

REMEZ: ALLEGORICAL INTERPRETATION

The shapes of each of the four types allude to parts of the human body, as the Midrash suggests *[Midrash Rabbah, Emor 30:14; Sefer ha-Bahir]*. The round esrog resembles the heart, which symbolizes the seat of emotion. The straight lulav resembles the spine, which is understood as a vertical channel carrying messages from the brain to the body, connecting the upper and lower dimensions. The leaves of the hadasim have the shape of eyes, symbolizing the faculty of sight. The leaves of the aravos look like lips, symbolizing the faculty of speech.

Binding and holding these four symbols close together, and reciting a blessing over them, we invoke the unification of self that we aspire to achieve through the course of the holidays. What we see (what comes into us from the outside), and what we say (what goes out from inside ourselves), should be consistent with the messages we receive from our higher, spiritual knowing—and our emotions should be aroused accordingly. Everything within us should be in harmony, and all directed upwards to

Heaven. Therefore, we hold the bundle upright when we make the blessing, directing all our faculties towards the Divine Unity beyond us.

Remez: ALLEGORICAL INTERPRETATION		
Species	Body Part	Element to Harmonize
Hadasim	Eyes	What is seen
Aravos	Lips	What is spoken
Lulav	Spine	Knowledge
Esrog	Heart	Emotion

DERUSH: HOMILETIC INTERPRETATION

Corresponding to the four categories of natural substances mentioned above, there are four developmental stages among people in relation to Torah and mitzvos [*Midrash Rabbah, Emor, 30:12; Kli Yakar, Vayikra, 23:40*].

The nourishment of Torah develops and transforms the way we think, our internal reality, or 'taste'. The beautiful practices of the mitzvos develop and transform the way we act, which is our appearance, or 'aroma'. Although a transformed mind ultimately transforms our actions, and actions can also reach inward and transform the mind. Still, we can generalize and say that the focus of Torah is inner development, while the focus of mitzvos and beneficial actions is outer development.

Some people have already transformed themselves inwardly through Torah knowledge, as well as outwardly through mitzvos and acts of generosity. Like the esrog, these people both 'taste' and 'look' good. They are notably transparent to the Divine Presence.

Some people are like a lulav—they have the good 'taste' of higher knowledge, yet their external behavior and appearances are not so 'aromatic'. Their knowledge and deeds are not yet in synch. Some are like hadasim in that their actions are beautiful, they are pleasant to be around, they do many mitzvos, and yet they are empty of Torah. Their minds and inner state have not yet been transformed; their 'taste' is not yet refined. Finally, there are some people who are like the aravos, having no aroma or taste. They are 'raw material', ready to begin the path of self-transformation.

When we take all four species, hold them together and recite the blessing, we realize we must bring together and unify these different kinds of people to properly sing Hashem's praise. We can do this by judging each person according to his merits. Similarly, we must unify the different stages of development within ourselves—we must judge ourselves favorably and include every part of ourselves in our divine service, regardless of our apparent stage.

Derush: HOMILETIC INTERPRETATION		
Species	**Area of Transformation**	**Stage or Area**
Esrog	BOTH KNOWLEDGE & ACTION	BOTH INTERNAL AND EXTERNAL DEVELOPMENT
Lulav	KNOWLEDGE, WITHOUT ACTION	INTERNAL DEVELOPMENT PREDOMINATES
Hadasim	ACTION, WITHOUT KNOWLEDGE	EXTERNAL DEVELOPMENT PREDOMINATES
Aravos	NEITHER KNOWLEDGE NOR ACTION	NEITHER; AN UNDEVELOPED STATE

CHAPTER ONE

SOD: SECRET

The Arizal relates the Four Species to the four letters of the name of Hashem, the *Yud-Hei-Vav-Hei [Shar ha-Kavanos, Sukkos]*. Rabbeinu Bachya says that the Four Species actually embody the Name of Hashem *[Rabbeinu Bachya, Vayikra, 23:40]*. This is consistent with the Midrash: *"Esrog is the Holy One...Hadasim is the Holy One...Lulav is the Holy One...Aravos is the Holy One [Midrash Rabbah, Emor, 30:9]*. When we hold the lulav and esrog, we are holding in our hands, as it were, 'a part of Hashem'.

The three hadasim correspond to the letter Yud of Hashem's Name. Yud, as a word, is spelled with three letters: Yud-Vav-Dalet (י - ו - ד). These three letters in turn symbolize the sefiros or attributes of chesed (kindness), gevurah (restriction) and tiferes (compassion).

The two branches of the aravos correspond to the upper Hei of Hashem's Name. Hei is spelled with two letters: Hei-Hei (ה - ה). These two letters symbolize the attributes of netzach (confidence) and hod (humility).

The long, straight lulav corresponds to the long, straight letter Vav (ו). Both symbolize the attribute of *yesod* (foundation and connection) and the masculine energy of the Divine.

[Rabbi Menachem Rekanti, writing a few hundred years before the AriZal, teaches that the lulav is tiferes, the three hadasim are chesed, gevurah and yesod, the esrog is malchus and the aravos are netzach and hod *(Ta'amei ha-Mitzvos)*. Above, we are following the Arizal's understanding, which is very similar to the Rekanti's, yet slightly different.]

The esrog corresponds to the final Hei (ה) of Hashem's Name, and thus it embodies the attribute of *malchus* or 'kingship' and the feminine Divine Presence. The *Rekanti* writes that the esrog and malchus also symbolize *K'neses Yisrael*, the Community of Israel, the presence of Hashem in the world, or the reality of the world today.

Malchus is the crown of *yesod*; they are two parts of a unified process. This is why the Torah calls the esrog *"the beautiful fruit of the tree"[Vayikra, 23:40]* — and not just the 'beautiful fruit' — since the "tree" is yesod, and the "fruit" is the malchus of yesod. When we bring the lulav and esrog together in our hands, we are demonstrating this natural unity of malchus and yesod. We are joining the 'masculine' (the deeper reality of 'redemption' in our world) and the 'feminine' (the current, unredeemed state of the world).

Sod: SECRET		
SPECIES	LETTER OF DIVINE NAME	SEFIRAH/DIVINE ATTRIBUTE
HADASIM	YUD	CHESED/GEVURAH/TIFERES
ARAVOS	HEI	NETZACH/HOD
LULAV	VAV	YESOD
ESROG	HEI	MALCHUS OF YESOD

The three hadasim, two aravos, one lulav and one esrog, add up to seven elements. The number seven corresponds to the seven Ushpizin or spiritual 'guests' who visit our Sukkah over the course of Sukkos: Avraham, Yitzchak, Yaakov, Moshe, Aharon, and Dovid. The Ushpizin also correspond to the seven emotional sefiros. The three hadasim correspond to the three Patriarchs, Avraham, Yitzchak and Yaakov, who embody the qualities of chesed, gevurah and tiferes, respectively. Avraham is chesed, unlimited kindness and giving. Yitzchak is gevurah, intense discipline and introversion. Yaakov is tiferes, blending 'giving' with balanced discipline.

The two aravos correspond to Moshe and Aaron, the great prophets. Prophecy is rooted in the sefiros of netzach and hod *[See Rabbeinu Bachya, Vayikra, 23:40].*

The lulav corresponds to Yosef, who embodies the focused energetic expression of yesod. Yesod brings correction, balance, unification and alignment to all the other sefiros. Thus, Yosef brings correction and unity between his brothers, as well as between his brothers and his father, and he orchestrates a re-alignment of all the citizens of Egypt.

Chapter One

The esrog corresponds to Dovid. Dovid is the King, the expression of malchus in the world. As malchus is feminine, the 'receiver', Dovid, receives seventy years of life from Adam.

Species	Ushpizin (7 Shepherds)	Sefiros
Hadasim	Avraham/Yitzchak/Yaakov	Chesed/Gevurah/Tiferes
Aravos	Moshe/Aaron	Netzach/Hod
Lulav	Yosef	Yesod
Esrog	Dovid	Malchus

When we bring together the lulav, aravos, hadasim and the esrog, we facilitate the alignment and joining of all these divergent energies.

SOD SHEBE-SOD: SECRET WITHIN THE SECRET

The 'secret within the secret' is that there is no secret. In the words of Rabbi Chaim Vital, "The peshat, the 'literal interpretation of Torah', and the remez are one" *[P'si'osav Shel Avraham Avinu, Os 62]*. The GR"A says the true peshat is in total alignment with sod *[Even Sheleima, 8:21]*. In life, sometimes the deepest secret is revealed within the seeming mundane experience or object before you; the omek or 'depths' of the peshat are the omek of the sod.

Chasidus explains that not only are we creating yichud or 'unification' in the world by binding and taking the lulav together with the esrog, but on the peshat level, each of species is already an expression of mystical unity. We only need to look carefully at the arba minim to notice this.

The lulav is a frond of palm leaves before they have opened out. Torah calls this *kapos timarim*. *Timarim* means 'palm leaves', and *kapos* means 'together'. When we look at a lulav, we see that under certain conditions it can spread open and divide into many leaves, but now it is in a unified state.

The Torah says that on Sukkos we should take a *pri eitz hadar*, literally, a beautiful fruit of the tree *[Vayikra, 23:40]*. Our sages say the word hadar alludes to *ha-dar b'ilano mishana l'shana*, or a fruit *"that lives on its tree all year round" [Sukkah, 35a]*. The nature of the esrog is to grow year round, which is very unusual for fruit. *Shana*, 'year', comes from the word *shinui*, 'change'. A year is a full cycle of changing seasons. By growing all year round, the esrog not only defies change, but it grows throughout them all, unifying all aspects of the year into one beautiful fruit.

Proper hadasim have three leaves arranged in tiers of three. That is, there are three leave clusters emanating out of the branch at the same level on the branch. This is a clear visual demonstration of the idea of unity.

Aravos grow in tight, unified clusters, which, according to halacha, indicates that they may be used for Sukkos. It is said that aravos grow like 'brothers', and that in fact is their name in Talmudic terminology *[Likutei Sichos 19, p. 358]*. The word *aravos* has the same root as the word *areiv*, blended together. Again, even the surface appearance of these plants reflects the secret of unification.

A COMBINED MAP OF THE FOUR SPECIES				
	ESROG	LULAV	HADASIM	ARAVOS
FORM OF BENEFIT	TRANSPARENCY	SATISFACTION	BEAUTY	UTILITY
AREA OF HUMAN TRANSFORMATION	INTERNAL AND EXTERNAL	INTERNAL	EXTERNAL	UNTRANSFORMED
BODY	HEART	SPINE	EYES	LIPS
LETTER OF THE DIVINE NAME	HEI	VAV	YUD	HEI
SEFIRAH	MALCHUS	YESOD	CHESED/ GEVURAH/ TIFERES	NETZACH/ HOD
BIBLICAL FIGURE	DOVID	YOSEF	AVRAHAM/ YITZCHAK/ YAAKOV	MOSHE/ AARON

Unity in Motion:
INTENTION IN WAVING THE FOUR SPECIES

In the previous chapter, we explored the positive imagery of the *arba minim*, the four species—such as the letters of Hashem's name, a unity between people, a unity of the masculine and feminine aspects of reality, and the enlightened attributes of the Patriarchs. Another type of imagery in the arba minim is that they are weapons of battle. The lulav looks like a sword.

Our sages tell us that once we pass through the time of judgment spanning Rosh Hashanah through Yom Kippur, we proudly parade with upright lulav, showing that we have been victorious in judgment. *[Tanchumah Emor, 18, Midrash Rabbah, Vayikra, 30]*. Rabbi Moshe Chaim Luzzato, the *RaMCHaL*, elaborates: through waving the lulav, we are holding up an emblem or weapon that disquiets our spiritual enemies. *[Derech Hashem, 4:7]*. In other words, the arba minim can be seen as instruments of cutting away negativity.

With this additional type of image, we can now move on to discussing the na'anuim, the wavings, or movements, of the arba minim, with their intentions and meanings.

THE NA'ANUIM

The Gemara *[Sukkah, 37b]*, says that we should wave the

arba minim back and forth, and up and down. Today the custom is to wave them in the four cardinal directions, plus up and down—six directions in total. The *Ramah* writes, however, that *b'di'eved*, or after the fact, any form of waving is sufficient to fulfill the halachic requirement of na'anuim.

According to the Rambam, the na'anuim are part of the mitzvah of taking the lulav and esrog: "Once one [merely] lifts these four types…he has fulfilled his obligation, so long as he lifts them in the manner in which they grow [i.e. upright]….[However,] the proper performance of the mitzvah is to lift a bundle of the three species in one's right hand (the lulav, hadasim, and aravos) and the esrog in the left, and then thrust them forward, bring them back, lift them upwards, and lower them, and wave the lulav three times in every direction. *[Hilchos Lulav, 7:9]*" Thus, the *l'chat'chilah*, or a priori fulfillment of the mitzvah, is with the na'anuim. *[See the Rosh on Sukkah, 3:33.]*

SPIRITUAL FUNCTIONS OF THE NA'ANUIM

The Gemara *(Sukkah, 37b)* relates: "Rabbi Yochanan says, We wave them back and forth to [honor] Him who owns the four directions, and we wave up and down to [honor] Him who owns the Heavens and the earth. In the West [Israel, west of Babylon] they learned: We wave back and forth to counter harmful winds (from the four directions) and up and down to counter harmful dews."

These two opinions reveal a positive and a negative reason for the na'anuim. The first is to show the Oneness of Hashem, which pervades all directions and dimensions. To declare Hashem's Unity in all creation, and as the Chinuch writes to remember Hashem is all of life. The second is to negate negativity, to nullify negative forces. The latter could mean to purify the atmosphere of physical pollutants, or to purify the psychic and spiritual environment from negative influences.

The Midrash *(see Tosefos ad loc, and Aruch haShulchan)* says the waving has to do with Hashem's judgment of

Creation: we wave the lulav to show that the earth is dancing, alive with singing Hashem's praise: "Then the trees of the forest will sing for joy."

Our personal energy-field or nefesh extends six feet around our body. If we are susceptible, and if we have spent time around negative and pessimistic people, their energy-field can intermingle with our own and have a detrimental effect on us.

When we wave the lulav and esrog in the six sectors of our energy field, we cleanse our immediate environment and create a protective wall around us. This relates, again to the teaching in the Midrash, which says that holding up the lulav is like holding up a sword, demonstrating our victory, and having cut negativity away from our lives.

Purifying and elevating the six directions of the psychophysical and spiritual world, creates great joy, and we may be moved to dance. Dancing, lifting the feet is a natural expression of elevating the world, defying gravity. The nights of Sukkos are full of dancing, a tradition going back to the *Simchas Beis haShueivah* ceremony in the Holy Temple. The culmination of this process of purification and elevation is Simchas Torah, when we victoriously lift all of ourselves, and all of Creation, up to Heaven.

BACK AND FORTH

In each waving of the lulav, there are two movements: outward into the specific direction, and then inward, back toward one's body. The Maggid of Kozhnitz *(Avodas Yisrael)* explains that the outward movement is about pushing something away, and the inward movement is about *yichud*, unity, drawing in.

As such, the two basic intentions are actually four. Within the intention of showing Hashem's Unity in all directions, the outward movement pushes aside the kelipah that prevents us from being aware of Hashem's Unity. The inward movement draws recognition of Hashem's Unity into our lives.

Within the intention of purifying the atmosphere and

its influences, the outward movement can be seen as pushing aside negativity, and the inward movement as pulling positive influences toward us.

DIRECTIONS

There are a couple variations in the sequence of directions for the na'anuim. We will discuss the sequence of the Arizal. The Arizal's sequence is to first wave the arba minim to the right, then to the left, then forward, up, down, and finally backward. The custom of Ashkenazic Jews who do not follow the Arizal's sequence is forward, right, back, left, up, and down. If your custom is the latter, you can still adapt the following intentions and kavanos.

According to all customs, we begin by facing East. Each one of the six directions embodies one of the six emotive *sefiros*, or attributes.

The right represents the sefirah of chesed. Left is gevurah, front is tiferes, back is yesod, up is netzach, and below is hod. The center, being the person waving the arba minim, is malchus.

South – Right - Chesed
North – Left - Gevurah
East – Front - Tiferes
Up - Netzach
Down - Hod
West- Back- Yesod
Center – Malchus

The seven emotional sefiros are:

Chesed – kindness; love
Gevurah – strength; restriction
Tiferes – beauty; compassion
Netzach – victory; ambition
Hod – devotion; humility
Yesod – foundation; relationship
Malchus – royalty; receptiveness

Chesed, or kindness and love is the right column, the act of giving and extending. On the left, is the restrictive column of *gevurah*, strength and inwardness. Between chesed and gevurah is their synthesis, *tiferes,* or beauty and compassion, the middle column. Tiferes is giving with a sensitivity of to the needs of the recipient, how much the receiver could and needs to receive. This is true compassion, which creates harmony and beauty, and is the synthesis between giving all and withholding completely.

The outer implementing sefiros, are as follows; on the right, the expansive column is *netzach*, or victory and ambition. On the left column is *hod*, or devotion and humility, and in the middle is the unifying agent, connecting the giver and the receiver; the idea of *yesod*, or foundation and relationship.

Malchus, or kingship, is receptiveness. It represents the vessel that receives from the preceding nine sefiros.

Surrounding Space and Inner Space

When the six directions symbolize our surrounding space, our body represents inner space. The acts of waving are then a process of assimilating the six outer points into our inner self, or integrating the six sefiros into malchus.

Surrounding space is the idea of *makif*, light that is still beyond us. The six-sided structure of the sukkah also represents makif. The acts of dwelling in the sukkah and of waving the arba minim are both processes of bringing makif down into *penimius*, our inner reality. The entire festival of Sukkos helps us take all the inspiration, commitment and glimpses of transcendence experienced on Rosh Hashanah and Yom Kippur, and bring them inside, into the tangible and practical side of life.

The *s'chach*, the material forming the roof of the sukkah, the makif of the sukkah, is a representation of the makif energy generated by the inspiration of Rosh Hashanah and Yom Kippur. The numerical value of the word s'chach is 100. The Arizal writes that the s'chach is the makif created by our heartfelt cries, and the 100 shofar-blasts of Rosh Hashanah.

According to the Zohar, the s'chach is a manifestation of the smoke of the *ketores*, or incense, which burned by the High Priest in the Inners of Inners, the Holy of Holies of the Temple on Yom Kippur. Today, when there is no actual Temple and no physical High Priest, our own inner work on Yom Kippur, in the inner, inner recesses of our soul is the service of the ketores, and the smoke aroma is the inner perspiration that is produced through our hard labor which becomes the s'chach of the sukkah.

This rarified aroma arises from the most transcendent, angelic moments of our Yom Kippur fast, and ascends to the Divine Presence. On Sukkos, this spiritual aroma descends again and hovers above us as the s'chach, embracing our human state, as we enjoy food and community.

On Pesach, we perfect our inner space as we eat the matzah. On Sukkos, we perfect our outer space, as we envelop ourselves with mitzvos. Unlike any other mitzvah, we enter with our entire body and existence into the sukkah. When we enter a mikvah, the only other mitzvah we enter fully, we stop breathing—we cease being, so-to-speak. But surrounded by the sukkah, we allow the full array of natural existence: eating, drinking, studying, conversing, and even sleeping.

Interestingly, the Gemara *(Beitza, 30b)*, says that with regards to the esrog, every day of Sukkos is a separate day, since the mitzvah of lulav and esrog is to be done anew each day. The esrog thus represents *penimius* or the inner, the personal, the particular. With regards to dwelling in the sukkah (since there is a mitzvah to sit by day and by night) all of Sukkos is like one long day.

The sukkah is thus the idea of makif, surrounding and including all days. It literally surrounds all of us, our entire body, and symbolically surrounds all of Israel, as "It is fitting that all of Israel should dwell in a single sukkah." *[Sukkah, 27b]*.

The sukkah is therefore an intermediate level of makif, light of oneness that still needs to be drawn down further into penimius to be integrated. The arba minim are like an antenna that receives this hovering makif and channels it all the way down into the multiplicity of details of life. This is why many people have the custom to make the blessings over the lulav while standing in the sukkah.

DRAWING CHESED, LOVING-KINDNESS

Each time we wave the lulav in one of the six directions, we move it in that direction three times (3x6=18). Every day of Sukkos we perform the waving sequence four times in total (once before Hallel, when we recite the blessings over the lulav, and three times during Hallel). Therefore, every day there are 4x18 waves, equaling 72, which is the numerical value of the word chesed.

According to the Arizal, the *na'anuim* draw down *makifim* in the form of chesed. Thus on the first day of Sukkos, we draw down the chesed within chesed; on the second day, we receive the gevurah within chesed, and on the following days, the tiferes of chesed, netzach of chesed, hod of chesed, and the yesod of chesed. On the seventh and final day of Sukkos, called *Hoshana Rabbah*, or the Great Salvation, we receive the malchus of chesed, and in addition, we draw all the chasadim that we received throughout the entire festival, into malchus—into our everyday life.

The *Tikkunei Zohar (Tikkun 6)* says that the 72 na'anuim elevate the whole world. The GR"A explains (*ibid.*) that there are 70 nations, with their 2 primordial leaders: *Yishmael* and *Esav*. Our na'anuim, then, not only channel chasadim into the world, they also break the negativity of spiritual distortion in the world, and elevate all of human consciousness.

According to kabbalah, we should make the blessing over the lulav in the sukkah prior to the Shacharis service, and wave it there. Therefore, with the four times we wave the lulav in Hallel, plus this initial shaking, there are a total of five sets per day. Five sets, times six waves per set, equals 30 directions, corresponding to the thirty blasts of the shofar which are the basic halachic minimum on Rosh Hashanah.

These shofar blasts shatter all concealments and sources of negativity, rectifying chesed, and bringing life to the world.

A Mystical Correspondence with Chanukah

The *Rikanti* notes, that we wave the lulav and esrog in six directions for six days (the seven days of Sukkos, minus Shabbos, when we don't wave them), and 6x6=36. We also kindle 36 lights throughout the eight nights of Chanukah (1+2+3+4+5+6+7+8=36). Every Rabbinic holiday, is rooted in a Torah Holiday; Chanukah is rooted in Sukkos *[Sefas Emes, Chanukah]*.

The House of Shammai ruled that on the first day of Chanukah, eight lights are lit and every day they are reduced until the last day, when one light is lit. The House of Hillel ruled the opposite way: on the first day, one light is kindled and one light is added each succeeding day, until there are eight. One reason for the ruling of the House of

Shammai is that the candles of Chanukah correspond to the bullocks that were offered in the Temple during Sukkos. On the first day of Sukkos, thirteen bullocks were offered, and each subsequent day there was one less. The House of Shammai was drawing a parallel between Chanukah and Sukkos. *[Shabbos, 21b]*.

The thirty-six candles of Chanukah correspond to the thirty-six hours that Adam and Eve were enveloped in the light of Gan Eden—half of Friday, plus the 24 hours of Shabbos. Thirty-six is also the number of times that the word *ohr*, light, appears in the Torah *(Rokeach)*. By moving our lulav and esrog 36 times, we are transforming our mundane space into sacred space, a place where the pure light of *Gan Eden*, also known as the *Ohr haGanuz*, the Hidden Light of Oneness experienced by *tzaddikim* or enlightened souls is revealed. The na'anuim draw down and reveal this divine light, shielding and protecting us from all negative influences.

The numerical value of the word lulav is 68, which is the same value as the word *chayim*, life. The lulav draws down to us life force for the coming year. The 18 movements performed in each set of na'anuim also allude to the numerical value of the word *chai*, also meaning life.

The upright lulav resembles the vertebral column, which has 18 vertebrae, and the movement of the lulav indicates vitality, life-force. According to Halacha, the arba minim that we use must not be dried up—they must have some life-force in them. The *Rikanti* says the word lulav means *lo-lev*, he has a heart. The heart is our inner source of life; if someone is said to 'have a heart', he is alive, both physically and spiritually. The lulav thus channels the transcendent Divine life-force all the way down into our innermost penimius, the heart of our being.

Chapter 3

THE LULAV MOVEMENTS OR *Na'anuim*

How to Perform the Na'anuim

1. Stand facing East.

2. Hold the lulav in your right hand and esrog in the left, place them together. Keep them together throughout the entire set of na'anuim. (If you are left-handed, the esrog and lulav are reversed, with the esrog in right hand and lulav in left.)

3. Move the bundle to the right, away from your body, and gently rustle the leaves of the lulav as your arms extend fully. Then draw the bundle inward, touching your heart with another gentle rustle. Repeat this two more times, extending your hands to the right and drawing them back inward to the heart.

4. **In the same manner, extend your hands three times to the left, each time drawing them back to the heart.**

5. Do the same in front of your body, toward the East.

6. Do the same upwards, raising your hands. Depending on where you are, be careful not to damage the tip of the lulav on the ceiling or the s'chach.

7. Do the same downwards, lowering your hands. There is no need to bend your body down. The tip of the lulav should not be pointed towards the ground, since according to the Arizal, the lulav should be upright throughout all of the movements.

8. Do the same behind you, over your shoulder, or by swiveling your body around briefly toward the space behind you, while keeping your feet pointed toward the East.

In total you will have gestured with the arba minim in six directions, and three times consecutively in each direction.

CHAPTER 4

DIAGRAMMING THE NA'ANUIM

The Illustrated Guide to the Lulav Movements

How to Hold the Lulav and Esrog

fig.1; fingers covering the esrog

The top of the esrog should be held next to the bottom of the lulav.

When holding the esrog while making the movments and during hoshanot, the top of the esrog should be covered with the fingers.

When moving the lulav and esrog due west, the esrog should be uncovered.

CHAPTER FOUR

Stand facing East the entire time.

*fig. 2; The first set towards South
{your right}*

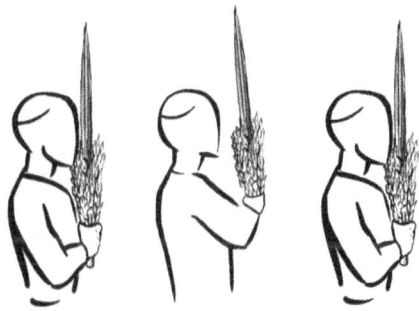

*fig. 3; The second set towards North
{your left}*

*fig. 4; The third set towards East
(in front of you}*

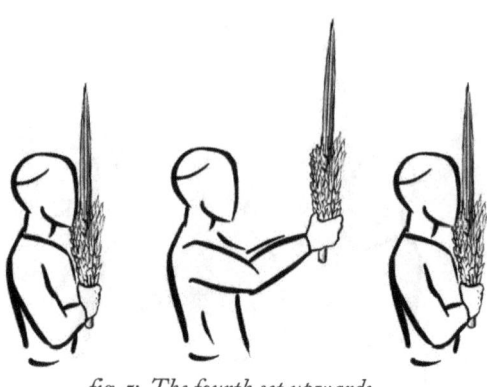

*fig. 5; The fourth set upwards
{above you}*

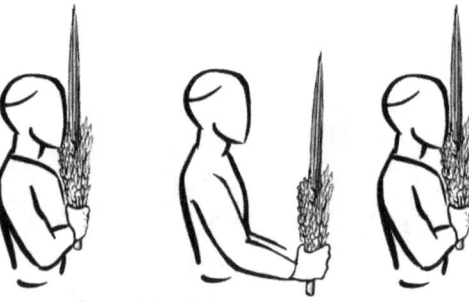

*fig. 6; The fifth set downwards
{below you}*

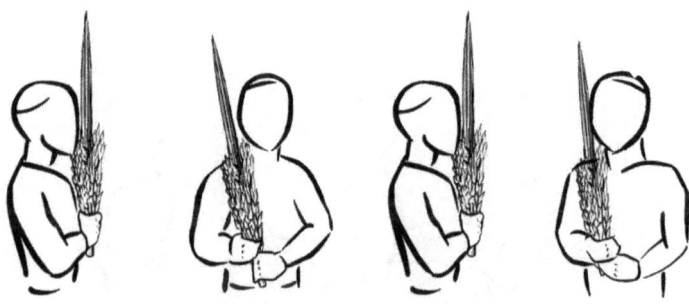

*fig. 7; The final set **twice** southwest (towards your shoulder and facing behind)
and **once** due west (fully behind your shoulder)*

KAVANOS
{Intentions}
1 & 2

As we mentioned, there are two basic intentions in waving the arba minim:
a) honoring or revealing Hashem's Unity in all directions and,
b) eliminating negative energies and influences.

The out and in movements comprising each of the six wavings represent pushing out or removing what is not good, and inviting in and internalizing what is good.

KAVANAH I:
Hashem's Unity

This kavanah declares that Hashem's Presence fills all directions:
'Hashem's Presence is above me, below me, to the right, to the left, before me, and behind me.'

Obviously, Hashem's Oneness encompasses all directions, and there is no need to itemize or list the directions where Omnipresence can be found. The depth in this intention, however, is to explore our own realization of Oneness. Where, within our personal attributes or sefiros, are we not yet acknowledging or trusting Hashem's Omnipresence?

With the outward movement we can contemplate our lack of Unity-consciousness in certain areas of life, and with the inward movement, we can bring in a greater level of Unity-consciousness in that area.

Accompany the movements with a silent prayer or affirmation, such as the words suggested below. As a prayer, you could say, "Hashem help me push aside…" instead of "I push aside…."

Face East, breathe, and settle your mind for a moment or two.

1. RIGHT / SOUTH / CHESED / חסד

OUTWARD MOVEMENT:
I push aside the 'concealment' involving my lack of recognition of Hashem's Hand in all my actions.

INWARD MOVEMENT:
I draw to myself the awareness that Hashem is One; Hashem is present within all my actions.

2. LEFT / NORTH / GEVURAH / גבורה
OR DIN / דין / HARSH JUDGMENT

OUTWARD MOVEMENT:
I push aside the 'concealment' involving my lack of recognition of Hashem's Presence within my 'harsh' experiences and states of contraction.

INWARD MOVEMENT:
I draw to myself the awareness that Hashem is One; Hashem is present even in 'harsh judgment' and states of contraction.

3. FRONT / EAST / TIFERES / תפארת

OUTWARD MOVEMENT:
I push aside the 'concealment' involving my subtle belief that Hashem is not present before me, compassionately guiding me, helping me move forward in life.

INWARD MOVEMENT:
I draw to myself the awareness that Hashem is One;

Hashem's compassionate guidance is in everything I experience, leading me forward.

4. UP / ABOVE / NETZACH / נצח

Upward Movement:

I push aside the 'concealment' involving my belief that I have reached my maximum spiritual ability.

Inward Movement:

I draw to myself the knowledge that Hashem is One; Hashem's Presence is above, always inviting me higher and higher, and opening greater spiritual levels for me in the coming year.

5. DOWN / BELOW / HOD / הוד

Downward Movement:

I push aside the 'concealment' involving my belief that in my 'lows' I am separate from Hashem.

Inward movement:

I draw to myself the knowledge that Hashem is One; Hashem's Presence is my ground, even in my lowliness and low states.

6. BACK / WEST / YESOD / יסוד

Downward Movement:

I push aside the 'concealment' involving my belief in the existence of accidents or random events.

Inward Movement:

I draw to myself the knowledge that Hashem is One; Hashem's Presence is always backing me up; Divine Guidance is behind every experience and there are no accidents.

CHAPTER FIVE

KAVANAH 2:
Pushing Aside Negativity

This kavanah is based on the Gemara quoted above that says we wave the arbah minim in order to disperse and eliminate negative 'winds' or influences.

Again, we will correlate the directions with sefiros and different areas of spiritual development. The inward and outward movements will again give us different angles on those areas of development.

Accompany the movements with a silent prayer or affirmation, such as the words suggested below. As a prayer, you could say, "Hashem help me push aside…" instead of "I push aside…."

Face east, breathe, and settle your mind
for a moment
or two.

1. RIGHT / SOUTH / CHESED / חסד

Outward Movement:
I push aside my negative attachments and dependencies on false love. I push aside any negative fear of love or relationship.

Inward Movement:
I draw to myself the traits of positive love, openness and generosity. I draw to myself loving relationships.

2. LEFT / NORTH / GEVURAH / גבורה

Outward Movement:
I push aside my lack of boundaries and discipline, and excessive generosity. I push aside my negative judgments, and any inability to judge properly.

Inward Movement:
I draw to myself healthy self-control, and the ability to judge with loving kindness rather than anger. I bring in awareness of my positive power, strength,

discipline, and also strictness and restraint when appropriate.

3. FRONT / EAST / TIFERES / תפארת

OUTWARD MOVEMENT:
I push aside negative 'integration'—my attachment to any objects or people in my life that deplete my physical, mental, emotional, or spiritual energy.

INWARD MOVEMENT:
I draw to myself positive integration and harmony, allowing me to observe everything and everyone with a holistic view, and to see the bigger picture.

4. UP / ABOVE / NETZACH / נצח

UPWARD MOVEMENT:
I push aside lack of confidence, low self-esteem, or confusion regarding my abilities.

INWARD MOVEMENT:
I draw to myself healthy self-esteem and confidence,

and the ability to overcome all confusion, obstacles and hardships.

5. DOWN / BELOW / HOD / הוד

Downward Movement:
I push aside my arrogance, insincerity and ingratitude.

Inward Movement:
I draw to myself the traits of humility, sincerity, and humble gratitude.

6. BACK / WEST / YESOD / יסוד

Downward Movement:
I push aside my fear of the past; I also push aside all attachment to self-centered physical intimacy.

Inward Movement:
I draw to myself a state of unity with my whole self, and self-acceptance regarding both my past and my present. I draw to myself the ability to have only positive, selfless, holy intimacies.

OTHER BOOKS BY RAV DOVBER PINSON

Rav Pinson's books are available in all fine book stores and on the web.

REINCARNATION AND JUDAISM:
The Journey of the Soul

INNER RHYTHMS:
The Kabbalah of Music.

MEDITATION AND JUDAISM:
Exploring the Jewish Meditative Paths.

TOWARD THE INFINITE:
The Way of Kabbalistic Meditation.

JEWISH WISDOM OF THE AFTERLIFE:
The Myths, the Mysteries & Meanings

UPSHERIN:
Exploring the Meanings of a Boy's First Haircut

THIRTY-TWO GATES OF WISDOM:
Awakening through Kabbalah:

EIGHT LIGHTS: *8 Meditations for Chanukah*

RECLAIMING THE SELF: *The Pathway of Teshuvah*

GARDEN OF PARADOX:
Conversations on Creator, Creaion and Consciousness

ABOUT THE AUTHOR

RAV DOVBER PINSON

Rav DovBer Pinson is a world renowned Torah Scholar, author and beloved spiritual teacher, recognized as one of the leading authorities of authentic Kabbalah and Jewish spirituality. Through his books, lectures and seminars he has touched the lives of thousands around the globe. Rav Pinson is the Rosh Yeshiva of the IYYUN Yeshiva and the dean of the IYYUN Center in Brownstone Brooklyn.

www.IYYUN.com

www.ingramcontent.com/pod-product-compliance
Lightning Source LLC
LaVergne TN
LVHW041458070426
835507LV00009B/658